## Contents:

| | |
|---|---|
| Chasing the Void | 7 |
| Listen | 8 |
| The Cross... | 10 |
| Strikes... | 11 |
| Golden Virginia | 12 |
| Voices | 13 |
| The Colours of a Planet | 14 |
| A Soulful Newcomer | 15 |
| The earth beneath | 17 |
| Time after time | 18 |
| Hope | 19 |
| Higher Grounds | 20 |
| Early Morning | 21 |
| In Conversation with... | 22 |
| Talking Blues | 24 |
| The turning Point | 25 |
| The Autumn Blues | 27 |
| Unusual Times | 28 |
| The Meandering Journey of a Poet | 29 |
| Recession | 30 |
| The Collage of "Mother" | 31 |
| Do you understand | 33 |
| The Ecclesiastical Echelon | 35 |
| Give me a room to rest in | 36 |

# Chasing the Void
## and other poems

## Oladele Oladeji

© copyright Oladele Oladeji 2009

All rights reserved; no part of this chapbook may be reproduced
in any way without the written consent of the author

*erbacce-press* retain © copyright of this chapbook
in its current format

Cover-design, editing and typesetting by

*erbacce-press* publications Liverpool UK 2009

ISBN: 978-1-906588-55-7

*erbacce-press* can be found via: http://www.erbacce-press.com

Oladele Oladeji was was born in Paddington, London in the early 60s. but grew up in Nigeria, where he originates from, and where he had had most of his education, including a B.A. (Hons) in Archeaology. He also worked as an actor for sometime. This is his first published collection.

This collection is dedicated to "Him" and "Them" and "Us", the Makers and Creators. Our Sojourners.

**Chasing the Void**

You were born the Child
Of a Mother, you grow, you reach
Puberty, you start to understand
Life, then your life gets pear shaped, you fall,
Flat on your face, you end up
On a doorway. You bounce back,

You try to move on, you do
Move on, your life gets bugged again,
Really bugged, you struggle to
Reach out, you struggle for money,
You struggle to keep up with
Friends, you make effort to keep
Appearances, you pick yourself up, and up
You go.

You get bugged again, and again, but you
Pick yourself up, chasing the void. But
The cycle repeats, smash, on your face again.
You struggle to buy a meal, you think twice for
The first cup of coffee in the morning, you
Look in the cupboard, and all you find is a
Tin of passion fruits, and a sachet of noodles.

You cannot be bothered, you do not have
To bother, cause you are chasing the void. You
Dream of a pint in the pub, or a shot of
Vodka and coke, or exotic Cocktails, a fantasy, it's all a dream,
It's all a dream whilst chasing the void. You wake up

In the morning, look around your one bedroom
Space, and all you see is a void, a space, a gap.
You gather your pieces, clear your whole mess,

Pick up your baggage's, and trash, wondering how
To stop the chase, how to fill the gap, how to
Chase the void, the void of shattered memories. Then

One morning, you wake up, walk down the road
To buy a pint of milk, you look down in front of you,
Unintended, unexpected. There in front of you
On the wet street is a poster drenched by the rain
Of the night before, reading –

"This is the end of the chase, the void has been filled"
A Memoire. Good luck, you can apply.

You don't understand the phrase, but you still
Pick up the poster, look at it as you walk along, wondering,
"I am not alone in the race" I have to stop
Chasing the Void.


**Listen**

Listen, listen to me, can you hear me.
Listen to my voice, I want to know you, I want you
To know me, listen. Listen, listen clearly, listen.
There is no time to waste, listen = (Voices)

Listen, i want you to feel me, to understand me beyond
what you see on the outside, listen, listen.
I want you to see the colours inside of me, the nerves in my
heart, the veins that transports my blood, listen. Listen clearly,

Can you hear me, listen -- (voices) Listen softly,
look into my eyes, i want you to see the messages in my head
I want to know you, every cells in you, every message
being transmitted, every thought you think. Listen, listen very clearly,
i want to understand every chain of thought, and you, mine.
Listen -- (Voices). Listen - ( Sounds and Voices)

Why should I feel for you if you do not care, why should i worry.
I cannot listen unless you listen, forget my colour, ignore my cultural gaps,
disregard my ignorance, but listen to my voice, and I will listen too
Think for me, feel for me, remember by good deeds, ignore
my anxieties, correct my mistakes, take me for who I am, and
i will learn to listen, always. I will learn to forgive, I will endeavour

to work with you, in rain and sunshine. I will learn from your
knowledge. Listen, please listen, don't go yet. I want
us to talk, to dine together, to drink together
to correct each other in times of difficulties, to learn to share,
to aspire together. No don't leave me, please, listen
listen, listen. What? Alright, suit yourself,

What? I cant hear you, What? What did you just say?
No don't do that, just listen. Please, listen to me, to them, for us
for you, for you future generation, and another, and another
and many , many generations. Please, please don't be upset
just listen, listen. Listen please, please listen to me.

Hello, can you hear me? Can you hear me? Listen,
wake up please, can you hear me, can you? ...
Hello, Hello, Hello == (Voices, strange Voices) - (Echoes)

Hello! ---
(Lone voice, sounds and Voices)

We are moving on.

## The Cross...

The Clouded Throne Stands
Him
Her
Us

The Mirror Shone. Welcomed Sits, called.

Beneath, troubled waters, Sunken
Men, and Women
He, above
Drops the Pyramid of
Existence
To
Reach and Charm
The Human Race.
"Come"

Come and dine, Here, Nothing Matters
Here, Peace is Supreme,
Here, Poverty, Sickness, death
Perishes,
Wealth does not matter, politics and economic gains, a thing of
The past. Peace reigns supreme, purity, an everlasting
Beauty.
Lust and Fame, a Vanity Fair. Here, pain is defeated, horror conquered.
Love is released, Pure Love. The newly Born are Made, the dead

Are Risen,
him, above the Cross, Manages,
Controls the Height of the Pyramid,

Dictates the Languages thus Spoken.
A voice,
A Spoken Word,

A Pitch of Sound,
The Genes, Gently Placed, and Compiled.

A Gift of Life, a Genius, a being, is moulded
A Keeper of Words, the Secret to Life Placed
In its Voice, our Coming and Going.
The Cross is Yours, Mine, Ours,
Theirs, for the Thoughts of Mankind, For our
Everlasting Existence, for ever, and ever.

The Cross remains Erect.


**Strikes...**

One strike, two strikes...
One strike, two strikes, and one more...
One strike, two strikes, and some more...
Two strikes, one strike...
One strike,
Two strikes,

Some more strikes, many more strikes, so many
strikes.
More,
and
more strikes, many more strikes,
A string of strikes, strikes, strikes, just too many strikes...

Bang!

No more strikes, either one, or two, nor many.
No more striking, no, no more strikes...
Nor a bang, no more banging, no more strikes...

No, no more...

**Golden Virginia**

Green and Golden Wrapper
Tobacco, so refined, so Smooth
You are.
When I stayed down and out,
To you only, I found peace.

To Smoke alone, is a societal disgust,
A Medical pain. To the shattered artist, to you
I sing praise.
Your fumes to my nostrils, is a touch
Of hope. For some, your sight alone to the
Bin it calls.

Your Green and Golden Wrapper alone
Is Art itself. For you a wretched Soul alone sings your
Praise.

Your taste on my lips concocted a taste of Gem.
For you, and us I Sing your
Praise.

When hardship rants his tunes above, to love
And hope a reject calls. O, however vain you
Are seen on earth, to you forever, your
Praise I Sing.

**Voices**

You came on a dark
Night, then took me on a journey
to melancholy.

You spoke, and travelled with me
Deeper to discover me ___ your melancholy.

At your height, you sang angelic songs,
You spoke the words of love.
Your dirge songs, you painted, not as
A dark sea, but as thousands of daffodils,
And millions of red roses.

Like the red, black dotted ladybird you
Made me fly, you washed my vision, you
Healed my pain and heartache.

As a beautiful tropical butterfly by the flowing
Stream, you made me see the colours
Of the world in my cerebral cage ___ Your voice.

Nay, at the furthermost end of my lifeline
You sang an awakening lullaby for me to return.
But you, you ___ the voice, and your voices,
Saved my life for not singing
The songs of Passover.

## The Colours of a Planet

The earth is round, there are seas and oceans.
The mountains are high, the valleys are low, sometimes.
The sun shines over us, the moon cries,
Its tears showering us, its fullness protecting
Us-humans. Its milky, creamy yolk covers
Us like an umbrella, the darkness begging to be seen.

The planet is red, sometimes we see it blue,
another time it becomes yellow, somewhere else
the planet is brown.

It has peoples, it has plants. Different species of animals
graze its foot, its natural forces displays prowess.
Many challenge its versatility, some just
sit back, and observe the changes.
Babies get born, its people get old and grey, then die. Fade away.
Some get older and see red, some get older and see the colour
Blue. Some see the darkness, some are just coming out of
Darkness.

Its Gods beckons to its own followers, its religions
Struggle to find its own Space.
Some dress in pink, some in white, some, multicoloured
Outfits, and some, just dress normal.
We see red, we see blue, some people see pink
And some see nothing at all.

We try to reconcile, some refuse to reconcile, some pray,
some do not pray at all, and some, just drift along ,
negatively, or positively..
I see black, some see the colour black, some do not see at all.

We cry, we laugh, some are in pain, some do not feel at all.
Pain or Love.

Some feel love, the pure red colour of love, poignant, real love
Deep love, the redness in love.

Its politics are sometimes real, some times, not real.
Power fails, power breeds, power conquers.
Sometimes, power is shared, and sometimes, there is no power at all.

I see yellow, we see brown, sometimes pink
Other times we see nothing at all.
Until one day, the planet will evolve into another planet,
And another, and another, and another.

A silent breeze whirls its way above, gentle,
and gradual, All the colours flashing, from red
To blue, to pink, and brown, and yellow.
No tears, no screams, just a darkness,
and a gentle sleep. A flash of light, and a gentle sleep
to say goodnight.

The planet, gradual in shape, size, and distance,
evolves itself, and we, its created habitats,
curl gently from our slumber,
to be greeted by a new day, a new beginning.
A new universe


### A Soulful Newcomer

A player of Languages
A player of Cultures,
A player of nuances and behaviour,
A player of Rhythms' and Rhymes,
A colourful player, a painter of values and norms,
From Poland to Russia, From Canada to Spain,
From Italy to the coast of Africa, from Britain

Back to Russia. A raw player, a Sharp observer,
A colourful interpreter.
The space was Historical, the atmosphere serenaded with Warmth.
The audience was a handful, but critical.
The Visuals stated the Colour of a thousand languages,

A meandering flavour of Liquor and diets,
A depicted beauty of our homes and ties.
So well carved were the words.
So well mannered were the represented.
So well painted were the locations.

A player of Languages, a player of Cultures,
A player of nuances and behaviour.
A player of Rhythms and Rhymes,

A colourful Player, a painter of values and norms.
She looked innocent and felt raw as she played.
Yet, a fiery beauty evolves that holds the onlooker.
Emotions eloping and Galloping like the Sea waves,
A beauty of States filtering onto our eyes,
Effortlessly, calmly and evocating.

From Russia to Spain, From Canada to America,
From Italy to the Coasts of Africa, from Britain
Back to Russia. Hence depicts the Colour of
A Soulful Newcomer. A raw player, a sharp observer,
Above all, a Colourful Interpreter.
Sharp,
Raw,
In fact, a Colourful and Mannered Player.

**The earth beneath**

In the heart of a busy, congested city,
the year 1991, on a long street sits a
bungalow barricaded by an unusual metallic
fence, its lower part in brick. The colour, a yolk, or
yellow touch. Inside, quite comfortable and
sparsely furnished, but tidy. Tiny specs of
bright light flashes at the back of my eyes like
someone overcoming a malaria bug, sometimes
the flashes are dark, as I lay curled up on the living room
carpet. On the other side of the centre table laid
The father figure, deep in his tireless world of law.

Its 0200am in the morning, dark, silent, with swift movements
on the street. There was a sudden yell from the local drunken
men, a sudden silence, darkness, red flashes, bright specs,
then a sharp plunge to the earth beneath. The walls distort my
vision on either side. Twenty feet wide, the dept, immeasurable.
A shiver, then flashes of lights surround me.

Blue, yellow, red, pink, and a heavy white flash. Father
figure appeared, still sleeping, as his spirit shines on me
like a new born child. The further i travelled, the darker
it becomes. Then came grandpa, not him but his coffin, a
black shinny polished wood with gold coloured frames. He
smiled and waved from inside as he led me on. But
at the bottom of the earth beneath, was bingo, the
long dead cherished dog from fishers lane.

Happy, vibrant, and bright. He led me back,
Jumping and licking my face as my eyes open to the realm of
a new beginning, a journey of courage, strength and hope, a
journey of life, and beyond. Sleep well bingo!

## Time after time

Time, think, time, think. Now or never --- Move.
A man must think -- Stop—
Time, for me, for you, for him, for them --- Think and Move.

For me, yes. For them, No, For them, yes, For us -- Stop and Think.
Time, yes, Stop, and think ---With time. With time, no, with time,
Yes --- Move. Yes, really move.
Let me think with time -- No. With time, = Stop. Yes, move beyond time.

Look back, think forward, move forward, and think backwards -- Stop!
Think forward.
Look deep, see deep, search deep, feel deep --- What?
I said, look deep, see deep, search deep, feel deep - Stop! Then move.

Time, think, time, think.

See, feel, search, look, always == Time after time.
I can see you, you can see me, we can feel you.
They can search for us --- Move, never stop, always move.

Think, stop, feel, time does not wait.
See, feel, think, search, look, look deep, search deep,
Find, feel and think, stop, don't stop, feel, never stop feeling.
Think, never stop thinking, time after time.

Season after seasons, moment after time, time after each moment.
Look, see, feel, find, cry, don't ever cry, cut, don't detach
Find, see, look, search, feel, == Time after Time.
Stop! Look beyond. Now and ever = Time after time.

## Hope

Forgive my misconceptions—
My ignorance is not a flaw but a misconception.
Every failure is a pivot to excellence---
Our attitudes says us, for us to see, for us to change,
For every mans progress, for the growth of nations.

Forgive my bad language, forgive my intolerance.
I want to know you, we want to understand you, and they,
Need to understand us. To understand them, we need to understand you.
Accept my shyness, I would respect your boldness.
We need to know your inner feelings, I will release my inner feelings.

I will like you to touch me, you must allow me to touch you.
Hatred is real, but for me, its tolerance, its love.
I will worry when you are sick and tired, I will care
when hope is lost. I will cry in times of joy, I will laugh to
Soothe your pain. Accept my ignorance, understand my
Shortfalls, and I, will revive your hope. I will run to bring us together.

I will fight to hold you on. I will challenge to see us grow.
We will struggle to save our country. we shall protect our countrymen.
As a strand I hope we stand, as a model, I hope for us.
In difficult times, our strength is tested. To defeat the wicked,
I hope it is. For now its time to think, i hope our dreams arises as wished.

## Higher Grounds

How do I begin to express this Burning Desire of Love,
Joy and Hope that Clouds my Imagination, even in times
When Societal imbalance and Human Delinquents, in these
Hour of Reconciliation and Restoration, Wrestles with
My Restlessness and Vigour to release that thirst, that thirst
That I have yearned for decades in hidden shapes and Colours,
In Closed Shutters that barricades that flow of juice
That he, the Gods of Art and creativity embedded deep Within
Its own Creation of Human Flesh, covering its Skeletal
Form with its inside pumped Full of the Blood, its nerves
And electrons changing places as I attempt my place
On Earth.

We all arrived here on earth on a Journey. Some will cover a few
Kilometres and return, others will keep travelling many more
Kilometres, and Accomplish their dreams and desires.
For Some, its just a few Yards to Higher Grounds, Many may join
In the race, But only a few might survive. The Eagle Flies
And takes refuge at the Pinnacle of the Highest Mountain, looking
Downwards to hunt its Preys. One mans dream is another's misfortune.
Another mans aspiration is the Dream for another Man.

As you dream and think about me in your silent Slumbers, so
Do I dream for a fellow Man to Touch Higher Grounds.
Its not a Pity that sometimes a man fails in his desires to fulfil
His Potentials, but it will be a pity not to acknowledge the
Efforts of a fellow man, great or Small, young or Old.
The Gift of the eyes is to see. The beauty of a mans Vision is
To first remove those Specs that Blankets the eyes, every Man peeling
Off their eyes Specs for us to abide on a further Journey
Beyond our Fragmented imaginations to cleanse Mans weaknesses
and Flaws.

I see you every day, I hear you all the time. You think of me when you
Talk around your dinner Tables, They ravel at your Creativity,
                                      and hear your name.
Some do not understand, Others try to understand. The King blows his
Trumpet to beckon the entrance of his Servants. You responded,
                                      They answered
I went through, Some Struggled to get through, others ran so fast
Before the Gate shuts. The King Bellowed again, and again, blowing
Passionately on his Golden Trumpet for every man to hear.

This Time, everyone went through, our Visions Clearer, our Thoughts,
Deeper, our Beauty, more Colourful, as we take our seats around the
Table on Higher Grounds.


### Early Morning

Oh how cool you are,
Early morning.
Your cool breeze slaps on my
Face, and brings me
To life. Everyday, every morning.

Your subtle feel means
You are awake to see
Me through the
Day. Another morning.

When you are sad, your face
Seems dull for us to
See, and admire your brightness.

In times like this you listen
To a gentle voice,
Screaming, "early morning,
Please, stop crying, wake up, we
Want a glorious day."

A sudden thought, and your eyes
Clears for us
To see your dimples
Through a clear
Sky.

Oh, early morning, how
Sweet it is to see
You again.
Until tomorrow morning, at dawn,
I say "Good morning
To you"
Early morning.


## In Conversation with…

You, Yes, You, Come back here, Where are you
Going? You cant run, why did you do it, yes, why did
You blow up Thousands of People, Why, why did you do it ---
                                        Extremist! Extremist!
Hey, You, Come back here, Why do you like making others
Life's a misery, That Old woman has worked all her life,

Why did you break into her domain, Why. --- Answer me, why.
You there, in dark Clothing, Yes, You, Why do you like
Robbing people. I am asking you. Is it for Pleasure or for a Kick, or that
You are just Stupid and Thick, hey, answer me---
You , yes, No, not you, Him, Him with the Thick Rimmed Glasses.
Now Speak to me, Why do you like Fiddling with minors, answer me.
You enjoy them? Hey, you get a Pleasure and Watch them
Cry, Watch them through a horrific Pain of a lifetime
Because of your Sick Mind.. Don't you think you should perish?
Don't you think you should rot in hell, struck by brimstones---
                                        Answer me.
You, yes, I am watching you, you do too much Drugs, and sell
                                      too much too.

Why, why do you peddle drugs, You have sent Mrs Wrickets Son
To rehab so many Times, his Brain cells are now as tiny and shrunken
Like a new born Chicken, you gave him the Chickens, you make
Him Clock every minute of the day, just for a few pounds.
                                Judgement is -Rot.

No, No, don't Sneak away, you Know its your turn to Rot in Hell
Why are you carrying that Gun, and That Knife, and the Crowbar, Why,
Why cant you get a job, settle down and have a family,
Why cant you go to college, or gain some skilled Trade, Why, Why
Cant you accept that she fancies Him more than you, Yes Why--- Come on
Answer me you Coward, answer me - Repent, repentance is not late.

Mr James Taxes that you have just Stolen, and Mine Too, and Mrs Wallard
In Flat 2009, and Many others we do not Know about, Why, Why did you
Do it, Answer me? As for you others, I am coming back, I am
Keeping an eye on you all, and I shall hit you very Hard.
Do you get me, Very Hard. Did you say Why? I will tell you why.
Because I am in conversation With, in Conversation With ---later.
Goodbye.

## 24
**Talking Blues**

Its Lancelot Andrews House, its summer, July 1992.
The long dormitory was full of Social rejects, turn-offs
Talking Blues echoes gently from a broken transistor radio.
It felt distant, but near. Enough to make "Him" drift smoothly.
"Him", lying face up on a single bed, smoking a cigarette.
Dave sits up on the opposite bed, the treasured sketch pad
Entrenched with sketches of "Him" in bed,
Smoking tobacco. Dave has a can of cider on the side,
                            sipping measured gulps.

At the far end, a group of mates argue on modern politics, playing cards,
and smoking joints amidst laughter, An interjected yell of
Talking blues erupts from the old radio, but disappears almost immediately.
It is bright, it felt dark, then suddenly it felt like a graveyard.
A mixture of horrid smell of unwashed bodies, and fumes from
                            smoking fills the air.
Encrusted stains of blood visible on the wall. Dirty beddings
                            graces the row of single beds.

Talking blues continues to fill the gap, with
"Him" absorbing, taking silent gentle moves, wondering
                            if "heaven" does exists.

On the left of "Him", the demon wobbles in bed, jerking from side to side
Eyes wide open, neither here nor there. He was wearing a
                            brown trousers, an
Oversized black shoes, with a long wavy unkempt hair. He
Stares at the naked image in the magazine for a while,
Talking blues still blaring, he rolls over, then the rotational
Bouncy movement starts, up and down. It stops with a sudden
                            orgasmic yell. Its over.

Dave laughs. At the far end the mates carried on, it meant nothing.
                            A daily routine, I suppose.
"Him" turns his back, shuts his eyes, and nods to talking blues,

Chuckling from the almost broken radio.
Where is heaven, "Him" thinks quietly, then comes the
Gentle outburst, "Send me home, make me see, I am
Crying in the name of the lord". Its beautiful,
Really beautiful, when "Him" reflects on talking blues.

## The turning Point

The Fear of Terrorism is eating our inside out
Either to Fly on an aeroplane, travel by Train or
Tram, gives us a Panic Thought, giving a Back Packer
A Watchful eye, or a Stern Glance has become a necessary
Reaction, sizing each other for acknowledgement , or power.

The state of our World economy is in Shambles
Our Ten year old understands the Principle of Money
Than we, the adult, the Parent, the Carer. Mans Loins has
Become Contaminated, its fertile eggs Mutated
By False Genes, the result, a production of Ferocious beings.

Our Youths and Teens, our well planed new Born
Created by its master, a produce of Mans Seeds, a Formation
Of our Chromosomes, delivered into a Confused
And Dysfunctional World , struggle to find their Space,
Their Childhood robbed, their purpose and Future Blinked
By a World of Greed and dissatisfaction.

Customer Services has Lost its usual Touch. A visit to
A high Street retailer has to end with a war of Words
With Floor Staffs ,or Manager, if you are not Buying, then
Do not ask. Again, Greed. Its about Sales, Money
And Profit Margins.

The Street corners are met by disillusioned youths, struggling
For Power, Fame and identity. Drugs being Exchanged
For Cash, Guns being Purchased for a few Pounds. Prostitution
Heightens, Teenage Pregnancy is at its Peak. What have we
Done Wrong, Where have we Gone Wrong, How did we
Go Wrong, What Shall we do now.
Religious Sects would not Stop Saying their Prayers, as they
Struggle bickering to have a Sit on the Management Committee.
An Honourable position, close to the Coffers. Grab, Grab, Grab
And Grab. Everyone is Grabbing a Piece of anything.
A piece of their own Flesh, others Sweat and efforts, the Wars are
Still eminent around the World.

The Monarchy is Silent, the Voices of our Parliament Rants
But Fades. Issues are trashed, the Debates are Steamy
And Vicious, but negotiations hard to reach.

What have we done Wrong, how do we cleanse the Global Recession.
How can we learn to Listen, how do we Compromise
How can we Learn to Reason, How do we offer a resolution.
How do you Feel now. Can our Siblings stop being Self Centred
When will our World start to Listen again.

## The Autumn Blues

Cool Breeze, Warm Breeze, Bright Days
Fine Evenings.
Beautiful Daffodils, Sweet Tasty Grapes.
A cool Lager for Pleasure,
For some, a Cool Cider, or Shandy
Or a Chilled White Wine.
And for some, a Glass of Rose
Or a well nurtured Glass of Red Wine.

Beautiful Days, Lovely Women
Well Toned men. Pale Skinned, Brown Skinned
Rough Skinned, Well Shaped Women.
The Parks are buoyant, the Streets Radiate.
Moods are Hyped, Businesses prosper,
Flights are at the Increase, Local Restaurants
Cash in on Thousands. The Rich
Smile, the Poor makes effort to look good.
Nice Tummies, ugly Tucks, Strait Legs, Long Legs
Pretty Faces, Men in Hipsters Wonder
For Friendships. Happy People, Lovely
People, Lonely People, Vibrant People, Strange
People, the whole world under one
Umbrella.

Nice tunes come to mind
Memoirs of the previous autumns springs to mind.
Gradually, gradually, and just gradually, the
Days roll by, the days roll by gradually.

Gently, just gently, to welcome us into the beautiful
Summer months, the months of joy, to many
The Months of Street celebrations.
The Months of Love, the months of reunion.
Until Winter sets in, to prepare
Us for the start of a new
Year to come.

## Unusual Times

There is a Great Feel to rare Moments.
Sometimes they are Funny, many a time, with
Laughter, big gestures and Salty rolling Tears.
Unusual times could be times of Celebration
A gathering of friends, acquaintances, lovers, more lovers
Relatives, and more, more strange relatives, Sometimes
Very Good people.

Times of unusual occasions are very pleasant, calling
For reconciliations, reminesance of the past
Frolics, mischief, sounding the voices and tones to
Recapture those special moments from a distant past.
Unusual times are beautiful, rich in its originality,
Fresh to its archivist, real to the listeners, a moment
Of comfort to its player, the narrator, leading us on to a
Special place.

Times of unusual events may be sad, may be catastrophic, may
Be of natural causes. Above all, unusual moments are to
Celebrate us, to recall actions, small or big,
A lovers cry for forgiveness, a recognition for a good deed
A lullaby to a toddler, or even a good laughter after a
Night out bouncing off jokes and silliness, all, and all
Of these are a recollection of our unusual moments, unusual
Occasions, our unusual times.
Great to recall, fun to resonate, lively to replay.

## The Meandering Journey of a Poet

He was born, a dark world ahead, he crawled
And Walked.
To the Seas, the sound of turbulent waves Sings
Its hymns, Wild and passionate to his ears to hear
And its Colour painted its love,
For him, to See, and his Mind, to imagine.

His anger, his jealousies, his hatred, his Kindness
And his Compassion, here begins.
The Voices speak.
For him, he visualised their thoughts.

Loud, but intense, buried within his soul, seeing his World
Painted before him.
He grew, he learnt, he withdrew, he expressed.
The World changed, his journey progressed. They, the overseers
Called. For him, he spoke the words from their eyes.

He wrote their Minds, their thoughts, he expressed their feelings.
Then they asked him to return, to narrate his troubadours
before their very eyes for them to see and listen.

They listened, endorsed, and then asked.
"Do you want to start all over again"
The Poet answered, "Yes, I will do it all over again".

**Recession**

A dark cloud engulfs us,
Far from our skies, lately.
Millions of bats hovering, the vultures perk, and eyes glued on
Our world.

Rats of different sizes clamour amongst us.
In Great Britain, to the dreamlands of
America, into the far walls of china, and the Berlin walls of Germany.
The African sunset cries like a new born baby
As farmlands perish. Its waters drains, its husbandries' getting extinct.

The Governor of the Bank of England

Sits, covered in hot sweats, shivers, and despair,
The colour of his skin changing to the
Tunes of its people's uproar and disgust.
Politics!

Politicians run riot, the mathematics, too complex to absorb.

I reflect on my o, levels Economics in tears.
Theories! Methods!
The Asian Theorist

Wrestles' in my dreams. In the mirror, transpired to the geniuses
Were
Formulas, figures, strategies, more formulas, and more strategies.

Mapping! Economic Mapping, Mapping! Economic strategies.
The air smells of

Homelessness, rage, hunger, starvation, deprivation, pain, anger,
                                    poverty, destructions,
And the Swine Flu.

Recession! Recession! Recession, who are you? This equals to,
Debates!/ Conferences!/ Seminars!/ The Parliament deliberates.
                                              The White house
Rants.
Recovery! Recovery, O I praise!
Afar,

As we stand, all I see is one man, and
The Moon shining through the dark skies above.
A Camera he holds,

With a single Ray of Light looking down
On earth, and its people,
It's full Beam Splashed like Artists

Paint on a plain Canvas.
On the right hand corner of the Canvas, stood an Altar

with

A Red Book titled,

"The Songs and Praises of the World"


## The Collage of "Mother"

Ebony Skinned you are,
A smile that kills, you wear, always.
Average height you are, a dark rimmed glasses, and a sense of dated
Fashion. That's you.
(Mother )
Transferred from you, to me, is a sense of fashion.
(My brown Tweeted Suit)

A body embedded in strength, vigour, for a decade I watched
You, your curious glances, as puberty set its rage upon me. You smile
As you admire my courage amongst my peers.

(You prepared me for romance, as you watch me woe,
  love, and make love)

Your delicate dishes, the savoury of utmost taste,

(From your mastered recipe, not one,
But many),
Such that trained my palette, such that shaped my body,
Such that shaped my mind.
This is your making.

(Mother) =

One more decade I saw you grow, your skin still glowing
Underneath the African Sun, your thoughts on us, shone like the colours
of the rainbow, your worries painted on the number of your wrinkles.
Your Body, still whole, for us.
(Your Creations)

Amidst hard times, your smiles still bears the colour of

(Hope, the Colour of your Strength)

Your determination exonerating, your feet, balanced to withstand

The darkest of times, the brightness of moments,

The dept of life's changes as reflected through us, your creation.
That's you.

"Mother"

Many more decades, erect you still stand, older and wiser,

You're Skin, still glowing under the African Sun.

For you, life loves, and celebrates. For me,

Your love, and being reminds me of

(Brown Tweeted Suit)

The one

I wore at Sea.
Its you.

"Mother"


**Do you understand**

    Like an Australian Kangaroo
    Nurturing and dragging its child around
    In the forest, such is the joy
    Of a mother the day she gives birth
    To a new sibling.
    Do you understand!
    Two decades later, that child is a man,
    Or a female, an adult. Then you
    Want to grow up quickly.
    You do Drugs, you drink alcohol
    Excessively, you break into cars, you do
    More drugs, and sleep around with
    Prostitutes, and sell your mothers
    Expensive jewelleries.
    Then your whole life is messed up.
    You lose hope, you sit in your stinking

Derelict space in the street corner,
You start to imagine the flat screen T.V
That mother bought, and you stole, you start to imagine
Yourself sitting by the dinner table
To a large bowl of rice, or bangers and marsh,
You start to see your loved uncles, your
God –parent with the lovely presents at
Christmas. You start to miss your
Loved sister, and brothers.

In the meantime, you have messed your life
Up, you start to smell, everywhere you
Go you leave your trade mark __ Stench, stinky Stench.
You start to get emotional, you start to
Cry your eyes out. You now want some
More drugs, and alcohol, you now
Want a mothers touch. But mother
Has lost hope in you. She will not have you back
Cause she will be dead worried you will
Take what's left of her, she does not want you
To pollute your brothers, and sisters, because you
Turned a failure. Do you understand! Do you really
Understand!

Now you want to break the habit, the terrible cycle, its too difficult
Cause you are hooked. You are a hooker on drugs!
You have become an addict! You go for help,
You cry for help, it beckons, then you mess it all up
By not attending sessions. Back on the game again.
They become sick of seeing your messed up face,
Your skinny, boneless body, your smelly
Fumes becomes upsetting, because you have giving
Up on life. Do you understand! Do you really understand!

You can become whole again, you can see that T.V again
If you want. You can smile at Christmas dinners
Again if you want. You can stop paying

The pusher for contaminated drugs if you want. Mostly,
You can see Charlotte again, if you really want her... Do
You understand! Do you really understand!
You can be loved again if you
want to be loved.


**The Ecclesiastical Echelon**

Some are called for Pastoral Duties, Most Spiritually
Inclined, for the Sake of Men, to Purify, to Guide its
Flocks to the Heavenly Place, the Kingdom of its Holy
Purifier, God patiently sitting to Proclaim the Judgement
Day. A few are Divine, not Priestly, not Sacerdotal, nor
Placed in a Pastoral position, but still Spiritually Famous, Shaped
And Formed to a Clerical Degree, their Tier Parallel
To most Religious Servants, Interpreting the Creators Messages
In a unique Credulous Form for a Moralistic Value in a
World Driven by Devious goals, Selfishness and Evil Spells.

The Dark Knight is Symbolised as Evil, an Antidote of
Rage, Death and Uprising, a Requiem for Societal Misfit and Waste.
But Still, a Knight of the Dark, on the Echelon Stage, has
A Place in the Futuristic Proclamations' of Mans Place in the Creators
Kingdom.

On Earth, the Spiritual Guidance, their Formation, Thoughts
And Feelings, Shaped to a Degree of a Divine Messenger, are Looking
At the World Through the Minds Eyes, a Gift, not deformed, but
Embedded in a Body and Soul Solely for a Purpose- To See,
To Hear, to Feel, to Receive and Preach its Messages to
The World in a Colourful and Spiritual Tone- Its Speech Real,
Their Words Divine, Most Devine I would say, as we Travel
Through time and Space to discover our Ecclesiastical Echelon.

**Give me a room to rest in**

In your curious mind, upon your silent heart,
Within the windows of your conscience, I
Dare to imagine your anger and pain. In the solemn
Thought of joyous moments, the surreal playful
Times that connects our being within our rooms.

The rooms which holds a clarity of dreams, the realities of
A constant, and steady hope we both venerate.
To not recognise your weaknesses will be my failure,
But to respond with care, love and sincerity
To your hearts music, your minds reactions and
The depth of your conscience will proclaim my declaration
For our reconciliation. Not just you, but us, both of
Us, so we can take a gentle step to see each other again.

Give me a room in your quiet place, that space that
You only can create, maybe at the far end, or the middle,
Maybe as a tiny spec that may grow with time.
And I, in my entirety, in my subtle, and wandering
Moments, in my conscience and understanding
Of you, of us, of what is left to rekindle a
Fierce bonding, I will, a beautiful reincarnation of a lost
And tireless dream, rebuild again. I will, in love clean that room over
And over, and over again, always, until the rage particles are cleansed
Within us, to give room for pure love, the sheer beauty
Of a Robin, the strength, resilience, and hope of conquerors.

Thus, is my hope, this is your beauty, my hope
When you give me a room to rest in.